www.finishinglinepress.com

THIRTEEN SEPTEMBER MOONS: A Love Story

poems by

James P. Lenfestey

Finishing Line Press
Georgetown, Kentucky

THIRTEEN SEPTEMBER MOONS: A Love Story

Publisher: Leah Maines

Editor: Christen Kincaid

Cover Art: Steven Sorman

Author Photo: Larry Marcus

Cover Design: Elizabeth Maines McCleavy

Printed in the USA on acid-free paper.
Order online: www.finishinglinepress.com
           also available on amazon.com

Author inquiries and mail orders:
Finishing Line Press
P. O. Box 1626
Georgetown, Kentucky 40324
U. S. A.

Table of Contents

For Earth

For Susan

FULL MOON OF REGRET

I regret last night I did not tell you
how much I love you.

How much your radiant
beauty means to me.

How your palette of warm colors
lights up my night.

I stare open-mouthed
at your marvels,
unique, so far as I can see,
in the universe.

I regret I only send back to you
an enigma, a made-up story,
a bit of rock and dust.

Though it is a love story,
for we both love stories.

Mine is of the sad man in the moon,
always loving, but always distant.

What I feel from the embrace of you
is so much more than I return—
your tides, your months of light
and dark, your moods.

Last night I rose splendid
on your horizon, full as I can be,
bleeding for you. And later
tried to light a path directly
to each of your eyes alone.
So you too could be illuminated.

Did you see me?

THE ISLAND MOON

You say you love islands.
Do you love me, an island?
See me, deserted, surrounded
by sparkling black water?

What one book
would you bring
to share with me alone?
What poem?
What song?

I am barren, barely a footprint,
a blank slate for your fevers,
your whirling imagination.
Freight me with your dreams,
your epic sadness.

I will always write back to you.

"HARVEST MOON"
"Come a little bit closer,
hear what I have to say." —Neil Young

I was born old,
with an old man's face,
a Neil Young face,
a glint of light
in my slant smile,
my moaning a song.

When we met I was old,
when we fell in love I was old,
and I am old tonight in love
with all of what you are,
your ice, your sharp peaks,
your warm oceans.

When we gaze at each other,
strumming our shared chords of light,
my beautiful back-up singers
purse their swaying lips—
Mars descending, Jupiter rising,
Venus embracing.

Because we all
"want to see you dance again,
on this harvest moon."

"MOONLIGHT LYING ON THE ROOM"
—Robert Bly

For those whose home is night,
the reward is silver bars,
carved by the windows,
lying oblong on the floor.

Do you see how heavy they are?
Their incalculable value?
They appear only twelve or thirteen
times a year, if not occluded,
maybe the day before, the day after,
enriching everything they touch.

It is said some creatures grow in moonlight.
Others, we know, live in its sway
of appearance and disappearance.

Like sun warms our knees,
moonlight lifts our heads,
in spite of all that is
gravity. It pulls us

away from the mass of us
into a common wish,
a simple plea, a swoon.

THE OCCLUDED MOON

How often you gather to celebrate
my fullness, your eyes
reflecting my light like silver coins.
How often I abandon you.

Like last night.
The table set, guests arrived,
windows thrown open to harvest
my light, awakening all of you
to a night of love.

Then the tumbling clouds,
the lightning, the thunder,
the tears, the thrilling wind
and stampeding waves.

Can't that be enough for one night?
Why did you believe you needed me?
And of course I was there all along,
the occluded moon.

"WITH ONLY TWO MOONS LISTENING"

—rom "Mr. Flood's Party," by Edwin Arlington Robinson

How much reflected light
dare I imbibe tonight
to gorge my gray eye
into double sight?

The way Mr. Flood
said two moons listened
upon his drunken night.

For me to see two earths,
what glory that stare would send,
two blue irises flecked by white,
two earths watching throughout
my happy drunken night.

But I know, no matter
what tankards of light
overflow your sun,
in the morning
there is only one.
And that one a fright,
lit up like a tart
"in the silver loneliness of night."

THE HUNG-OVER MOON

Sallow, sagging, hollow-eyed,
a vast dark circle around me, why
did I shine so bright last night?

An attempt, with all my being,
to penetrate your dark clouds?
Trying so hard to impress you,
crying all night into swirling
gusts of moody rain?

So I drank and drank, and drank
again of your mysterious spin,
traversing the entire night
open-mouthed, gasping at stars.

Until, pallid and exhausted,
I faded into the light
of another of your
blinding dawns.

THE ESCROW MOON

How long have you waited?
How many years?
What clouds covered you,
obscuring your bluest eye?

I was there. The tides knew.
And the fishes, the corals, the smelt.

But not you,
your private volcano spewing
its own misery of cloud.

Then, like a long-forgotten check
arriving in the mail,
the clouds washed away.
The palm trees at your feet
waved in the breeze, dropped
coconuts for you to eat,
the bread fruit trees
baked in the sun,
the waiting fish
leapt into your nets.

And the House of Love
reopened its doors.

SIREN FROM THE MOON

Every month in town,
at noon, the sirens
are tested, ripping the air
with terror.

My siren is pure light,
neither fear nor hope
but heavier, neither love
nor despair, all
the same great weight.

Yet your noon siren
scares me too,
all the way up here,
what you have done to yourself
already, what terrible more
you are capable of.

Meanwhile, I love you
without reservation,
my siren song pulling
you neither to sea stars
nor watery grave, but

Only an effortless swim on
priceless moonbeams,
easy does it all the way,
head up.

FULL MOON SHADOW

What do you think when
the person next to you
tonight, who startles you,
who frightens you, is you?
Is attached to your body
by the soles of your feet?

No matter how dark you are,
he is darker.

You just stand there, moonstruck,
as I circle my spotlight
around you like some all night
police interrogation,
and you lie and lie and lie.

You who gave up wonder
as a boy for man's work,
what do you say now
to the darker person next to you,
forever part of your life?
Whose mysterious story
must now
be told.

I make that story true,
with my one eye.
My shine.
Your howl.

THE MORNING MOON

You did not expect me, did you?
On the other shoulder of the sky
from where I glanced at you last night.

Tell me what you see right now.
I imagine a silken, pale blue sky,
gold sunlight raked across the grass,
perhaps a patch of drifting cloud
and wind rustling the sea. Certainly
squadrons of you as you extinguish lights
and move out slowly over the curve
of you.

And me, still awake, watching.
Wafer thin now, nearly transparent,
my gray, sad features blending
with the blue of sky.
I am disappearing, but still
with you, as I have been all night.

I know what you did.
How hard you partied,
your arguments, how you loved.
And I know your dreams.

THE GONE MOON

So much I have never felt.
Wind, what is it?
I see it rustling the leaves
of your forests, the surface
of your lakes and oceans.

Water, what is it?
I'd love to fall into it,
cool myself with its
apparent suppleness,
its depths.
Its shifting colors
alone are erotic to me.

Your expanding deserts
and dust are my familiars,
your shrinking ice cap
is how I feel when I turn
my back.

But the green and blue
and gold,
How can you stand
such beauty?
How dare you
unfold its ruin?

MEMORIES OF THE GONE MOON

That scrim of cloud at dawn
erases any trace of me.
Though I suspect the sun still paves
its roseate pathway to your door.

Exhausted, I will turn my side
away, then my back.
If you did not listen then,
you will not hear me now.

Will you remember my face,
my hollow eyes,
my howling mouth?
And what I said to you?

I spoke in arias of silver,
radiant choruses,
cascades of moonbeams.

When I return, it will be
nearly your Halloween.
When your children seek
not golden day
but silver night,
all of us wearing masks.

Look for me then,
and for my shadow.
In the meantime,
my love, try
to remember—

I do know desire.
Longing.
Emptiness.

After a career in academia, marketing communications and journalism on the editorial board of the *Star Tribune*, where he won several Page One awards for excellence, since 2000 **James P. Lenfestey** has published a collection of personal essays, seven collections of poems, edited two poetry anthologies and co-edited *Robert Bly in This World*, University of Minnesota Press. His *haibun* memoir, *Seeking the Cave: A Pilgrimage to Cold Mountain* (Milkweed Editions), was a finalist for the 2014 Minnesota Book Award. His sixth poetry collection, *A Marriage Book: 50 Years of Poems from a Marriage* (Milkweed Editions), was a finalist for two 2017 Midwest book awards. For fifteen years he chaired the Literary Witnesses poetry program in Minneapolis and led a summer poetry class on Mackinac Island, Michigan. As a journalist he has covered climate science since 1988. He lives in Minneapolis and Mackinac Island with his wife the political activist Susan Lenfestey. They have four children and eight grandchildren.